The Heavy Empty

David Icenogle

BookLeaf Publishing

Presentation by *BookLeaf Publishing*

Web: www.bookleafpub.com

E-mail: info@bookleafpub.com

ISBN: 9789357212397

First edition 2023

DEDICATION

To my mother and grandmother. Thank you for keeping my writing alive through encouragement. Thank you for keeping me alive through love.

ACKNOWLEDGEMENT

Thank you to everyone I've shared a moment with. Thank you to the people I've loved and hated. Thank you to cats for showing me everything I love about dogs. Thank you to dogs for showing me everything I love about cats.

PREFACE

"Think you're escaping but run into yourself. Longest way round is the shortest way home."
-James Joyce, Ulysses

"I used to be a crackhead. I still am one but I used to be one, too"
-Unknown

"Empty Between the Elms"

There was a spider web I marveled
hanging near the mouth of a trail.
It was a dreamcatcher with the wingspan
of a farmyard windmill sewed
between two elms.
The web was a wispy accordion
pulled apart by the trees.
The black and yellow orb weaver would sit
serenely in the eye
of its own storm, moving
with the waves of the wind.
Today a child destroyed it.
With a fallen branch he poked
where the spider was
and twirled it like a wand
conjuring a spell of annihilation.
The web was wrapped and collected
around the stick like gray cotton candy
in front of impatient children.
I wanted to ask the boy why he would do that
but I knew there wouldn't be any real answer.
Walking the trail I can't stop
thinking about the now empty space between the
elms
and how something beautiful,
something made with such care and labor,

something depended on so deeply,
could be torn away
in a moment
for no reason at all.

"Too Old for a Dog"

They tried to talk him into a home
or a dog.
He was 12 presidents old and has renewed his
license 14 times.
He's just trying to make it to another renewal.
He says the only thing in his life
that has never changed
is the DMV.
His wife's license has now expired
but she does not need renewal.
That's what has brought on the awkward talks
and sliding
of brochures and pamphlets across the table
as if it was an offer. Or a negotiation.
His children are retired and stuck looking back,
his grandchildren are stuck looking forward to
retirement,
his great grandchildren are stuck looking for
nothing,
and he is stuck looking at the end.
His only health problems are time and being
widowed.
Everyone doubts he'll make it to great-great
but some men are too stubborn to die
and teenagers make mistakes.

As far as death and retirement communities were concerned
he was past the bargaining stage
and had the finances for acceptance.
He wasn't going to a home because he still had one
and he was always taught to finish his supper.
His Will would be active before his will would be broken.
So then it would be get a dog, a rescue
from the silence.
He had and loved dogs all his life.
Because he loved them he wouldn't get one.
Because the dog would outlive him
and what would the dog do
then.

"Smoke Break"

He picks from the outdoor ashtray with a
shameless focus.
Fingers like fleshy scissors, pecking through the
chalky ash,
sifting through the pile of Marlboro corpses.
The filters of the smokes nearly fossilized
from the dried fire and winterized saliva,
now cemented to the tips from the cold night
before.
His hand like a beak of a bird,
diving for sturdy straw to build a nest.
Some filters were crushed hard enough to rip the
cotton guts
of the cigarette butt, revealing the whiteness of
the inside
before the inhale stained the innards
with a butternut squash smear.
His fingers dig gently,
trying to find a filter that moves the pile in a way
that exposes one butt with enough of a bone to
be smoked.
The fact that his lips will touch the residue of
some other's spit
does not concern him.

Nor is he concerned with notion that the crust of slobber
could've come from a person who's sick,
or that the rust of red around the filter may not be lipstick.
These concerns are a luxury of thought
that his mind can no longer afford.
His fingers, now dusted to a ghostly gray,
carefully peruse the desert of ash for a Camel
that was left unfinished because its owner
had to leave it for something the man does not have.
The man does not see himself as a scavenger,
but someone who has taken it upon themselves
to finish what others had started.
He doesn't believe this
but he still assigns this narrative to his craft.
It makes it easier to plunge his hand into that silver bird bath,
and dig through the ash.

"Sweet Tooth"

She smoked her teeth away
from the bubble, if you're a country club
member,
that's what the lottery faithful
call a meth pipe.
She's the attendant for the bakery at Walmart
and she's from a place so secluded
the people there think going to Walmart
is a special occasion.
Sometimes she doesn't bring her fake teeth to
work
as if she wasn't planning on smiling that day
but she always smiles
despite the memories she has
kept behind locked bathroom doors
and being fluent in garnished wages.
She's looks elderly but she's 54.
Retirement isn't in her vocabulary,
benefits are getting to take some of the leftovers
home.
She's got medical bills that will walk her to the
graveyard
because she wasn't insured for what would
break her
and some of her pre-existing conditions

go back generations.
She'll have a mobile home longer than she'll have a mobile phone
but she still smiles even when she can't afford teeth.
She'll tell people her teeth are missing
because she has a sweet tooth
which is true but not in a way they understand.
We all got a sweet tooth,
just some cause cavities that can't be filled
and hers were caused by a Snake River-sized canal deep in her roots
that as a child had her riding shotgun
trigger-happy to get loaded
with other secondhand smoke kids
who conceal-carried open arms.
Somewhere in the holes inside her she found
an off-brand Jesus. I hope it helps
because even though her life has been
one long Band-Aid rip
she's the sweetest thing in the bakery.
Her name is Sheila and last month she became a great-grandma.
She's not embarrassed of being that at her age,
she jokes and says that she's always been a great grandma.
I'll believe in miracles for her
and if she doesn't get what she wants out of this life

I’ll believe in reincarnation for her.
I don’t believe in prayer but I pray for Sheila,
especially her great grandbaby.
I’ll pray a whole yard sale rosary
so that baby can be the first
to learn to smile without
bracing herself for the grinding nights
that everyone before her
has accepted as life.

"The Gesture"

We lost a lake
to find a boy,
or rather, tried to find
a body.
They kept saying “boy” even while searching
the drained lake. As if he would see
another birthday after being found
in a puddle that was once a lake
by a volunteer with a rake.
The boy hadn’t made it to his braces yet
and was missing for as long as a pregnancy.
The lake wasn’t completely drained,
there were still ponds scattered within
the Grand Canyon of dirt. But
the local fishermen were angry
and it pains me
to admit that there was a small,
ugly but honest part of me
that could see their point because
the only chance slimmer that he was alive
was that he was in the lake.
It was less of a search and more of a gesture
because if you looked in the eyes of his parents
when the sun of hope was setting
and hope for their son became pretending

you would want to move mountains for them
or empty lakes. Maybe
all the cranky parents that weren't able
to take their kids fishing that summer
could reflect on the feeling of missing their
children
rather than missing out with them. Maybe
they could take their children out to what was
once a lake
and as they stare out at that hollow crater
they would hold their children
as if they would disappear
if they let them go.

"Panic Attack Protocol"

You pull your hair hard, elbows like antlers.
You gasp through your teeth, chest stretching
upward like a balloon being buried alive.
Your lungs are filling with hummingbirds and
heat.
Your heart is a running boat propeller that has
been pulled naked from the water.
You are on a carousel and can't stop.
You are suffocating on the air you're drowning
in.
Breathe in. Through your nose.
Let that chilly wisp crawl through and caress the
back of your tongue.
Let your chest fill like a fire hose being woken
up by water.
Breathe out. Through your mouth.
Drop your jaw like a drawbridge.
Release that train of fog through the tunnel of
your lips.
Breathe in. This has happened before. You have
done this before.
Breathe out. You will make it. You always do.

"Holding Cell #3, Codington County"

I would never spend time with Tennessee
outside of a jail cell.
That was his name
and he gave the state a bad one.
Neither of us should've been in South Dakota.
Besides hate, he was trafficking drugs,
trying to launder his addiction into profit.
I was there because everything was breaking
down except my car.
He had thunderbolts on his neck
as black as a night sky over Dachau.
His arm was a bone wrapped in skin
with barely enough room for the tattoo
of a woman on a stripper pole
with the word "HUSTLE" stamped below.
The ink woman's face was completely shrouded
in hair made of spiderweb.
He said it's because he's had to hustle
as hard as an ugly stripper.
Tennessee has the charm of a dental drill.
Pity isn't the right word
but I feel something for him.
He has the aura of an abandoned house
that has a foundation made out of
the losing end of wishbones,

covered in the graffiti of ignorance
that he now pretends was a paint job
he had chosen.
On his other string cheese arm
he has a portrait of his mom,
the only person he's felt love for
in his whole life, as he tells it.
Now I gotta tell you,
faces with realism are difficult
for even highly skilled tattoo artists
and nothing on his body
was made by an artist.
His mother's face looks ghastly and
shaken like a face leaning against a bus window.
He told me he thought he'd never shoot dope
in that arm because his mama would be
watching.
Eventually he did
and while it's been a long time since the drugs
felt good
he tells me the high is especially bad
when it's in front of mama.
Rugged living and low quality has made
his mother's face fade fast.
With the sadness of erasing
a future baby shower from the calendar,
he tells me
her face can't fade
fast enough.

"Beginner's Meditation"

The silence is loud,
the awareness suffocating.
Do I always inhale and exhale
this irregularly?
My eyes are closed
but somehow I can’t stop blinking.
How often am I
clenching my jaw this way?
Why is it a struggle
to just sit?
In the stillness
the automatic becomes arduous,
reflexes burdensome,
the light on what was unnoticed
burns.
I keep forgetting
what I’m coming back to.
I’m thinking of things to stop thinking.
My fingers have let go of the tip
that was holding my balloon of attention.
Back to the breath,
I’ve been holding it in again.
I don’t think I can do this.
I’m told I need practice.

I don't think my mind will allow this.
I'm told it will help me
and I need help.
Back to the breath.

"The Last Happy Hour"

If you stopped squinting, or cringing, or crying
you could see that his death from liver failure
was merciful
considering that every subsequent moment
from that point was going to be worse
as impossible as that seemed.
His skin had looked like a banana peel.
The spill of jaundice rubbed
the whites of his eyes with dandelions.
He was both emaciated and pregnant
while he laid in his final bed
like a fired shotgun shell.
People whispered about irony
in the way, towards the end,
he needed to drink not to die
otherwise the withdrawals would've shaken him
death.
It seemed, in his life, that from his very first shot
he needed to drink to live.
I remember sleepovers with his son.
He haunted the house when he wasn't there.
He was the only person I knew
who had a bigger presence in his absence.
Because when he was gone
we knew where he was,

what he was doing,
and nothing could stop it.
After the wake we drank at the bar
where he killed himself publicly.
No whispers about irony then.
But maybe there is no irony.
Maybe it’s the best we can do
because if you forget the past
you’re doomed to repeat it
but if you don’t forget the past
you’re doomed
to remember it.

"Arts and Crafts at the Psych Ward"

The colored pencils are pointless to use because
they're pointless.
It's part of protocol for us beltless bunch
so the pencils stay long and the crayons get used
to the knuckle.
They cut out many craft options because scissors
are off the table.
The uncovered clay gets dry and unusable
unless you smash and squeeze really hard.
And some do
but never for artistic purposes.
But most of what's inside us
doesn't come out during art therapy.
Dark and gray colors are rarely used.
No snapped brushes, no furious scribbling,
the watercolors don't come from crying
over spilled paint.
We don't lose our minds
if the tremors make us color outside the lines.
We don't turn paintings into papier-mache
from tearing it up in a fit of rage.
Mostly it's coloring in something already made.
Simple shapes, color by number, page by page,
no wrong way or right, easy and bright.

A brief reprieve from the overflowing conveyor
belt of anxious thought
or the agitated catatonia sitting like a frozen
wasp
or the tension of everyone
sleepwalking with restless leg syndrome,
emotional but medicated into drowsy volcanoes.
Then it's back to vacant stares at the TV,
watching like solar panels soaking up the noise
to kill
the mind and silence.
I don't know why
they don't leave out all the supplies
and make art therapy all day.
It's better than anything else
in this institutional Purgatory.
Sometime art therapy is the only therapy that
works.
Because sometimes therapy isn't about making
things better.
Sometimes it's about holding on when things get
worse.

"Walks of Life"

Some mornings I get the urge
to walk a dog I haven't had in years.
I would let her lead me
through the drunk breath of a summer dawn
before the sun was big enough to blister,
paws pattering on the foggy sidewalk,
the jingling collar, the wet panting.
I followed her
through the cracking and crisp daylight of fall,
legs crunching through the leaves that were
brittle
as the exoskeletons cicadas shed,
the jingling collar, the sighs through her snout.
She would guide me
through the winter sting and the cold
that showed us how much space our breath took
up,
feet silent on the snow,
the jingling collar, the train puffs of her lungs.
She would drag me by the leash
darting towards the blooming sun of spring,
paws pausing to sniff pollen and roll around
in the buzzing growth of grass,
the jingling collar, the gasps from dashing about.
I walk without her now

through the silence of every season
to the beat of solitary steps,
the jingling collar of memory,
too aware of the breathing I do
by myself.

"Alumni"

My grandma's brother had a full-ride
scholarship to Harvard. It became
an accelerated program for self-destruction,
double-majoring in alcoholism and clinical
depression.
If he enrolled in Harvard Law and Medical, took
his time
like a morphine drip, bought even the unrequired
textbooks,
he wouldn't have incurred a fraction of the debt
brought on by the bottle and the emptiness.
He was as brilliant as he was broken.
I've followed similar curriculum and younger
me
would've taken the burdens to be loaned
brilliance.
Now I know about interest, the way it
compounds
as years and afflictions grow with you, when
getting through the day becomes guerilla
warfare
between purpose and impulses.
Impulses are like Afghanistan,
the graveyard of imagined empires. You stop
romanticizing being a tortured artist when you

recognize waterboarding is not interrogation
because not all suffering leads to
the answers to your questions.
I don't want to be special anymore. I want
to read the fine print. I don't want to be
unique like a snowflake, I want to be
unique like a raindrop and just enjoy
the freefall from expectations. I don't want
to stand out like a fingerprint, I want to be
safe in an oven mitt with an appetite
as small as my reality. I'm tired
of disappointment and potential coming in
tandem.
I'll be content in the center
of a school of fish furthest from the sharks
that smell blood in my aspirations.
I'm an alumni of the same school my grandma's
brother
attended in his head. I hang
my diploma in a panic room.
Except I'm not brilliant like he was
but I get the burdens regardless and I'm never
paying off the debt.
So I might as well allow myself
to dream.

"Second Opinions for Self-Portraits"

She makes me nervous
how quickly she reaches for her phone
when she sees a sunset.
As if beauty is so scarce in her life
that she's got to capture it
like sunsets don't happen every day.
She watches hope like my dog watches me
when I go to work and thinks that I'm leaving
forever
again.
She holds happiness like a butterfly in a Mason
jar
and always forgets to make holes for air.
Some people are so used to the current of
suffering
that when they're tossed a life preserver
they pop it with their teeth.
Because the hunger is like an anchor,
they are sailing by the feeling
of their sinking empty stomach
when all they were ever told was not to eat
before swimming
and don't accept yourself too quickly
or you'll get the bends.

Her phone is full of second-hand sunsets
and deleted pictures of herself,
only the ones she didn't like,
which is all of them.
The snapshots she takes of herself are vanity projectiles
she shoots into the void, hoping someone will see the tracer
of the comet that is burning so desperately.
Some people don't need to be told they're beautiful,
icicles and fallen feathers can be beautiful,
they need to be told they matter.
She ain't broken
she just needs someone to listen.
I will listen
because I too squeeze the life out of moments of joy
and have jars full of dead monarchs.
I will listen because I've been keeping distance.
I've been hugging people
like a scarecrow, holding people
with the tenderness of a beer koozie.
I've been drinking diet misery from the fear of full flavor.
I tell her to talk like a let go balloon
and I will listen like a cloudless sky.
Because we might be fighting the same demons
so I ask her to speak of the devil

so it shall appear
and maybe together
we will be strong enough
to beat him to death.

"Singer's Block"

I wish I could sing.
Even when I sing in the shower the shampoo boos.
The only note I can hit is puberty.
So I need words, analogies, metaphors, similes, context.
I'm tired of needing the crutches of context.
I need to express the spiral fractures in my restless legs
and I wish I could just show you
the exposed femurs without x-rays.
I want a voice that would point under the muscle
to those snapped pieces of chalk
so I wouldn't need to give you a doctor's opinion
on why I can't walk.
I get cutters. I wish they would stop. But I understand.
I wish they could sing
and have a straight-to-the-vein, uncut, unfiltered
form of expression without all the pain,
no more razor blade cursive, just a chance at a melody
spiked with some beauty
and a pinch of artistic flair

instead of waiting for catharsis from a therapist's chair.
I wish they could put down the knife,
pick up the mic
and sing brokenness into beauty.
I know I can sing, but not beautifully,
because I got this thing
that's small in my head but big in my heart
it's a small cost that I can't afford
like a tear in a bungee cord,
pride.
Pride with a splash of self-hatred and nausea
from the vertigo of being so self-conscious.
So I will not sing,
I won't even whistle
past the graveyard I've buried myself in
and I will have to write my epitaph beautifully.
If I could sing
I would only sing the lyrics I have wrote
and I have a feeling
that then
I still couldn't sing because
the lyrics would never be enough.

"Pretty Homeless Women"

I've been told there's no such thing
as a pretty homeless woman.
Yet here one is
on the corner with a cry for help
carved into cardboard.
According to many people who never
give to the homeless regardless,
this is a scam. A con. A kick to the money clip,
stealing change from your wishing well.
As if your empathy was going to be audited,
as if giving to the homeless has anything to do
with money.
Last time I checked, she asked for my two cents,
I didn't ask for yours.
If this is fake and she's method-acting a meth
addict,
she's impoverished, just in a different way.
Which some would argue is worse.
I would argue they've never been homeless
in a Minneapolis winter.
This woman shouldn't be homeless, allegedly,
because she should have other options,
financially.
While loving a man for shelter and security
isn't a homeless Minneapolis winter,

it is still a pretty
cold way to exist.

"A Lesson in Therapy"

When I was 14 I had a therapist
who related every one of my hints for help
with a story about
him.
His credentials and length of practice
mixed with his white sideburns
told me this profession was not his first choice.
Or maybe it was but he thought he could only
reach
financial peace of mind with 2.5 kids
from a corporate ladder
and that these things would fix
what he missed.
I started to become his therapist.
My afflictions were merely launch pads
for opportunities to show me his wounds.
His attempts at relating his life to my issues
became sloppier.
Plugging in mismatched extension cords
covered in stripes of duct-tape
come to mind.
His correlations from me to him became more
nondescript, forced.
Book reports I wrote about books I never read
come to mind.

There were many billable hours where I only
spoke for minutes.
He was helping himself. I was learning how to
keep to myself.
But our sessions were lessons
on how to keep an affected, frustrated, and
confused boy
alive inside the body of an older man.
He taught me that the art of suppression doesn't
need practice
and that childhood trauma has no expiration
date.
I learned it's never too soon to start dealing with
the past
but it will always seem like
it is too late.

"Out-of-Pockets to Pick"

They tell me
the copay for my medication is only
a hundred and fifty dollars.
The best way to measure privilege
is the way people use the word "only."
They tell me
I should be relieved
because without insurance it would've been
eight-hundred.
Why not make it a million?
Everything being articulated is all artificial
anyways.
They tell me
never, never, never
stop taking your psychiatric medications
abruptly
unless you can't afford them apparently.
I'm already buying off-brand, generic food
just to pay for the off-brand, generic
prescriptions,
maybe I could afford the one-fifty
but what I can't afford is the uncertainty
because last month it was one-twenty.
Spare me

the carpet-bombing of jargon that you think
will bully away my questions.
"It's complicated" ain't an answer
especially when it's on purpose.
Here's something not complicated,
people die without insulin
so don't intimate that this is negotiable,
don't intimidate and call it consensual,
and don't boast about what insurance has saved
me
when it's all Monopoly money.
I've spent way too many lunch breaks on hold
just to be told
I should've had an ailment that's in-network.
My patience has met my out-of-pocket.
I just want it to make sense.
If an apple-a-day keeps the doctor away
then this system is an orchard
rotten to the core.
It has the bedside manner of a buzzsaw.
And no
I can't tell you how to fix it
but that doesn't make me or it less broke
so I'm going to keep pulling fire alarms
if ya'll keep blowing smoke.
Why does every provider invite
an elephant into the room
that never forgets
pre-existing conditions.

So keep telling me how much money it's saved
me
and why not make it a million
because none of it makes a difference
when the insulin runs out.

"Canine Custody"

When everything ended
and we turned each other into memories,
she got the dog.
I felt lowly like a starfish, an ashtray stain,
my spirit brittle like curled leaves.
I should've fought harder for her,
the dog I mean.
She deserved a struggle, an effort,
something more than a car ride and goodbye.
I waved a white flag tied to a tail
between my legs, a sail
to a boat tied to the dock,
a clock with hands tied to the time
I stopped counting the second
chances I passed up.
When everything was over
and we turned each other into regrets,
I got a dog.
I made a promise
that this time I would not let someone
take a part of me
when they left.

"The Elderly Walmart Greeter"

He doesn't ruin my shopping experience,
he ruins my living experience.
When my partner and I walked into
the dog whistle static buzzing from
the florescent-light tidal wave
and aircraft carrier-level AC,
I saw him and had to excuse myself.
I wept in a bathroom stall
which I assume
many employees do on break.
They shouldn't breakdown
on their breaks.
Cry on company time, make them pay
you for the misery.
I couldn't meet eyes with him. I looked away
from his nametag. I don't want to know his
name.
I don't want him more real to me
than he already is.
He smiles like a hostage at faces sunken into
phones.
He is too old to chase shoplifters, too invisible
to try to check items and receipts.
I can but won't imagine the circumstances

that brings him to his role as a human
welcome sign, a breathing mannequin.
How does he do this, second by second,
40 hours a week, with only two fifteens and a 30
to take a breath above water?
But what if he'd shoo my pity away
and tell me that he's fine with his reality
and ask what does my deep fear and sadness
for him
say about
me?

"The Cancer Club"

Outside my apartment there are buckets of sand
and ash.
These are where residents discard the shell
casings
of cigarettes after they've turned
their cowboy-killers to ghosts.
Where Camels are buried in tiny deserts
with whatever else that didn't disappear into the
atmosphere.
They exchange small talk and burn chalk sticks.
The state tax on packs keeps rising
but the only thing that changes
in their hand is the brand.
Some say they're too old to quit,
some say they're too young to stop.
The residents that smoke
know each other better than the ones who don't.
There is community in what the higher horses
call "the cancer club."
The smoking section doesn't pay attention to
ivory towers,
they just burn them and blow away what's left.
Each of the butts in the bucket
represent a conversation, spoken or not.
Some dialogues go so deep

they last packs.
Some discussions get carried across
an entire carton.
Relationships get birthed from the butt bucket,
secrets get buried like ash in sand,
stories drift from secondhand.
I quit smoking years ago
and it is not the nicotine I miss.
It's too bad we have to kill ourselves
just to get to know each other.

"The Life of a Tree"

I wondered how trees die of age.
Placing my hand on the scabs of bark,
the wrinkles of mother nature,
I imagined a tree running out of time.
The burden of the seasons hummed from the
heartwood.
The trunk ached from traveling lifetimes
without being able to leave a single footprint.
But the grass that was baptized in the tree's
shade
saw the steps.
How many times did the tree have to watch
the clingstone peaches drop from its branch,
only to be carried away by scavengers
or melt from the heat of time into ground rot.
Every branch has twigs, every twig has
budscars,
every budscar an echo from a song of something
lost.
I wondered if trees remembered.
It looked as if the tree's crown was buckling
under the gravity
of its own memory.
But the roots under the horizon of land

spread powerfully and directionless through the airy soil
like a cluster strike of bolts driving through the dirty clouds.
My feet could feel the horsepower of those roots digging.
Digging to keep up with the burial of wounds left by the winters.
Digging deeper so that the tree can keep reaching towards the sunlight.
As the struggle of standing becomes harder to bare,
the tree is held up by the embrace of the canopy.
The brittle leaves cradle each drip of rain more carefully.
I wondered if a tree ever rests.
Because despite the weariness of its wood,
and the weight of the wilderness,
the tree still extends an arm so that the birds can sit.
Their nests will always be safe there
and in return the birds sing.
The hatchlings are taught this the moment they wake into life.
So that the tree, unable to leave its place in the ground,
can live throughout the forest
and be remembered with the wind
that carries their song.

www.ingramcontent.com/pod-product-compliance
Lightning Source LLC
Chambersburg PA
CBHW051739130826
49812CB00033B/931
9789357212397